HOW TO GET A GIRLFRIEND

TIPS ON HOW TO BE A MAN AND GET THE GIRL

CALVIN DALE

Contents

INTRODUCTION

Carrying on with the single life can be fun, however at one point, you should get a girlfriend. Actually, quite difficult, correct? In reality, you have a superior opportunity to get a girlfriend than you naturally suspect! From internet dating to approaching young ladies IRL, we'll walk you through the best techniques to begin finding and being with the young lady of your fantasies. Peruse on for a total aide on gathering new young ladies, further developing your being a tease game, and landing more dates with the young lady you like.

How does one acquire a girlfriend? I won't bother going up and asking any questions. It's really awkward.

Yes, after about third grade, approaching someone and asking them to be your girlfriend no longer works.

You don't "get" a girlfriend. Someone chooses to become your girlfriend. So, why might she choose to be your girlfriend? Think about the other side: What leads you to decide that you want a girlfriend? I'm going to guess something along the lines of, "You're attracted to her, you enjoy her company, you feel cushy, romantic, or sexy feelings toward her, etc." Therefore, it stands to reason that that is what would entice someone to become your girlfriend.

When a woman is attracted to you, likes you, enjoys your company, has romantic feelings for you, etc., she may want to be your girlfriend. So, the question is, how do you evoke those feelings? That is a significant inquiry. Most of the time, a person's first attraction is based on their looks and charm. Develop your social skills while looking your best.

You can attract a little bit more serious interest by interacting with enough people to demonstrate that you are interesting to them and compatible with them. However, this varies greatly from person to person, so I cannot offer any generic advice.

CHAPTER ONE

YOUR PURPOSE: FOR WHAT REASON DO YOU NEED A GIRLFRIEND?

Do You want to Get a girlfriend for the Right Reasons? This is a significant question to pose to yourself while you're hoping to attract ladies. The truth of the matter is, in the event that you're attempting to get a young lady for some unacceptable reasons, meeting ladies and dating will be a difficult, disappointing cycle. This chapter will inspect a portion of those horrendous purposes behind needing a girlfriend, and tell you the best way to beat them. Thus, attracting a girlfriend will turn into a simpler, more pleasant experience.

1. Attracting women to show off

At times a person is just keen on attracting ladies in light of the social approval it gives. He wants an alluring woman on his arm that he can showoff to friends and, family, and on-lookers. He thinks people will think more highly of him when they see that women want him.

Be that as it may, this mentality makes it hard to draw in ladies in any case. Ladies need to be something other than an item for a person to flaunt to his friends. In the event that this is the primary inspiration a person has for drawing in ladies, ladies will not want anything to do with him.

You can change this disposition by embracing the contrary attitude and investing wholeheartedly in being single. Embrace the demeanor of "No doubt I'm single, and a lady must be damn good to change that". Fortify that conviction by spending time with friends (guys and girls) who feel that same way. At the point when you never again feel that requirement for social approval it will be a lot easier to get ladies intrigued by you.

2. Getting girls for a confidence boost

A few men use relationship as a method for estimating their own self-esteem. A person like this will attempt to get a girlfriend just to demonstrate to himself that he merits something.

Yet, on the off chance that you're reliant upon interest from ladies to feel better about yourself, drawing in ladies will be darn-close to unimaginable. Ladies are not drawn to needy men. Women want confident men who already love their life.

To draw in ladies then, at that point, focus on making a daily existence you love. Invest energy doing exercises you appreciate (join a sports league, take a class, learn a new skill, etc.) and keep yourself healthy through diet and exercise. This will assist you with building confidence and feel good about yourself. When you're ready to completely partake in your life no matter what your dating circumstance, you'll transmit energy and fervor. This will get ladies to see you and make you more alluring to ladies immediately.

3. Wanting women out of spite

A person could say he needs to get a girlfriend yet when he checks himself, he understands something unimaginable - that he dislikes ladies. He resents the ones who dismissed him previously and needs to draw in ladies simply to refute those young ladies for turning him down.

Assuming that you attempt and attract ladies while clutching this hatred and outrage, you're facing a tough conflict. Regardless of whether you get a lady to like you it's inevitable until this disdain emerges.

Guys who find themselves irate and angry will benefit by building confidence and developing a surer mentality. You can do both of those things immediately by taking the time every day (or one time each week) to record your little triumphs - the things you got along admirably and beneficial things that happened to you. Develop that uplifting outlook by zeroing in on what's great in your life and what you bring to the table. This will assist that indignation and hatred with vanishing - making you more alluring to ladies.

4. Doing whatever it takes to make a girl fall in love

Then there's the person ready to do everything under the sun to get a young lady. He will do and be anything that he needs to make a lady experience passionate feeling for him.

This is a horrendous mentality to have for attracting people for two reasons. In the first place, ladies need a man with respectability who represents something - not a mat they can walk everywhere. Second, there will in general be a hidden common agreement that accompanies this disposition. This person is basically saying "I'll take the necessary steps to fulfill a young lady so that she'll cherish me." This demeanor isn't simply ugly to ladies, it's contemptible and manipulative.

Rather than being the mat, be the confident man women want. Turn into a man with principles that makes ladies pursue him. How? Begin by getting some margin to record precisely the very thing you need from a lady and a relationship. Then, when you go out and meet ladies, don't agree to anything short of what you need. Having this outlook and these principles will make you more appealing to ladies and is the way to getting ladies to pursue you.

CHAPTER TWO

REASONS YOU DON'T HAVE A GIRLFRIEND

You're single, yet you wish things were different. You might want to have a girlfriend. You're restless for that serious relationship that will be it for you — yet regardless of the amount you attempt, it simply doesn't appear to work out.

We should move the self-evident. We should accept for the time being that you're as of now "putting yourself out there" and "trying to ask ladies out." How about we additionally expect you keep up with essential degree of cleanliness and prepping, and you dress like in some measure alright.

You take care of the fundamentals, so we should focus on what else may turn out badly.

There are numerous approaches to expanding your own bliss. For the vast majority of us, the experience of heartfelt love is up there with pizza on the rundown of "things worth living for". In the event that having a girlfriend isn't your thing - congratulations! It's genuinely something amazing characterizing what you need from life and afterward making that reality. This chapter isn't really for you. In any case, if having a girlfriend is something you're prepared for, here are justifications for why it may not be working out:

1. You're focusing too much on yourself

Assuming you're single and asking "what's up with me?" - your focus is completely off-base. I see guys set all their focus on their own bodies or list of qualifications with an end goal to show up more appealing in view of some distorted rationale they've assimilated from our wrecked picture fixated culture. Be that as it may, truly, I've not even once dated a person because I was super into his forearms or in light of the fact that he worked in finance. What's more, in the event that a lady is just keen on you because of that - she's not keen on who you really are past how she can address you to her loved ones. That style of relationship will feel truly shitty actually rapidly, on the grounds that it's inauthentic.

Consider it - you notice people since they check on you, listen when you talk and pose inquiries about your life. It's a shared trade, yet that is the manner by which you really begin shaping relationship. So, stage one - quit agonizing over yourself, begin figuring how you can enhance her life.

2. The only time you meet women is when you're drunk

You and your friends might get dependent upon a few outright tricks on your evening out in the town, yet you realize the entertaining thing about wearing a traffic cone on your head and heading back home across the Harbor bridge at 4am? In a real sense, it's just your friends that think that it is entertaining. Furthermore, that is something wonderful. Be that as it may, before ladies who don't enjoy the benefit of realizing the complex, sincerely profound, physically in charge being you truly are - you're simply one more person spurting lemon juice into his eye at the bar.

3. You haven't really asked her out

I have brilliant, amusing, appealing person friends who say their most terrible trepidation is getting rejected. I get it. Presenting yourself to someone else by saying "hello, you're cool, we should hang out... and I don't mean in a dispassionate way" can be terrifying in light of the fact that you need to show someone else you have genuine sentiments which is counter to the reserved energies you've endeavored to develop.

Yet, measurably, you're bound to go out with a young lady on the off chance that you really ask her out. On the off chance that she says no, it's generally not personal. Be generous and continue on.

4. You're waiting for the perfect girl

Breaking: she doesn't exist. There's no such an amazing concept as a 'perfect' lady (except Rachel McAdams and Amy Schumer, if you're reading, please ignore the previous statement). On the off chance that you're sitting tight for a glorified indication of your next partner to coincidentally find your life, plan to die alone.

Everybody has great characteristics, so center around those. Try not to focus on what an individual can't give you. By simply integrating this one simple Jedi Brain trick into your life, you will extraordinarily expand the quantity of ladies you're viable with.

5. You're not offering anything

The premise of numerous a human relationship is essentially value-based. Ladies need to invest energy with guys because they receive something in return. Furthermore, I don't mean retrograde thoughts of offering ladies monetary assistance, despite the fact that liberality might mean material liberality occasionally. No - the top things a person can offer ladies are generosity, their insight and their time. Likewise, sexual chemistry. Also making us laugh. Also telling us we're pretty when we're feeling shit. See? We're really not asking for much.

6. You have a bunch of insecurities that you haven't dealt with

In the event that you're uncertain about your miniature penis or the reality you're in a lot of obligation, you want to manage this at this point. However long tell the truth and forthright about the fact that you're a vegetarian or anything that it is certain individuals could see as a dealbreaker, the ideal individual won't mind.

Feeling like you're 'not exactly' is especially predominant in a culture that underscores a thought that man must be Richard Branson levels of successful with the body of an extra from Magic Mike. Prepare to have your mind blown. You're enough similarly as you are. Taking a stab at personal development is beneficial, however sort out what you really can change, and bury the hatchet with what you can't. There's nothing more engaging than an individual who's OK with what their identity is and isn't attempting to be something they're not.

7. You don't focus on one woman at a time

You keep many conversations going simultaneously, with various ladies, and not even one of them is only a friend — you transparently flirt with them all.

You go on a first date, and it works out positively, yet rather than asking her out again one weekend from now, you plan one more first date with another person. You simply need to see what you could been passing up prior to putting additional time and exertion into that first relationship. It's no biggie. You can constantly return to the first lady at whatever point, right?

Indeed, ladies don't find it provocative when you carry on like a diverted canine, pursuing any squirrel that crosses its way. In the event that your objective is a serious relationship with a serious girlfriend, you need to focus on each lady in turn. Invest your energy conversing with her, getting to know her. In the event that the first date worked out in a good way, ask her out on a second date as of now.

Ladies could do without trusting that a man will come around and begin offering them the consideration they need and merit, they become weary of hot-and-cold way of behaving and surrender.

8. You're too impatient.

You're finished being single. You need a girlfriend — tomorrow. So, you come on come on too strong for first dates. You pine over ladies you scarcely know, you let your heart throb for them even before you know whether both of you have any potential at all. You're the encapsulation of the frantic male.

You frighten ladies off with how tenacious you are. You text them the entire day until they begin contemplating whether you have a daily existence. But it's not hot to seem to be on the off chance that you have nothing better to do than to focus on one individual day in and day out. Focus is great, obsession and fixation are not.

9. You're not learning from your mistakes

You've had connections previously — yet it's not your fault they finished (some of them seriously). You did literally nothing off-base. Your exes are insane, every one of them. However long you won't concede — and gain from — your slip-ups, you will keep on rehashing them, and your connections will keep on experiencing the normal, worn out issues you should have fixed quite some time ago.

There's no genuine development without an exhaustive assessment of your flaws. It's the manner by which you sort out how you can improve sometime later.

10. You don't see what a catch you are — so you self-sabotage.

You have some work, and you don't live with your folks. You're shrewd. You know how to convey an intriguing discussion, and you can make individuals chuckle. Not constantly, but rather frequently enough.

A lot of ladies would be fortunate to have you, however since you don't completely accept that yourself, you don't act in like manner. You incline in on your indecencies, and don't give your virtues enough credit. You twofold down on your blemishes while sabotaging your most desirable characteristics.

You damage your connections before they can appropriately start, and you burn through your time pursuing ladies who don't merit you, since you don't figure you can improve.

It's time you check out what you bring to the table for a partner and perceive the worth you can add to someone's life.

11. You don't give the ladies you date a fair opportunity

When they do or say something you could do without, you lose it. You anticipate that they should be awesome, and your relationship to run as expected, so you have little persistence to figure out things, to arrange, to think twice about. You don't allow them the opportunity to reschedule, to apologize, to attempt once more — you boot them out at the first misstep.

You end up back at the dating market nearly when you leave it, feeling more deterred than you ought to. Your view of the absence of important partner is totally contorted by how much you expect of individuals you date. It isn't so much that your standards are high, is that you're expecting to date a romanticized lady who leaves to satisfy you, without any requirements or norms of her own.

Connections are tied in with changing course as you go. It's basically impossible to have one without pardoning your partner missteps and allowing them a subsequent opportunity.

12. You expect a lot from a relationship.

You liken being single with being hopeless. You let your dejection characterize you in a manner nothing else at any point has. The main salvation for you is a partner.

You need to observe that unique individual who will make your days more brilliant and your evenings more joyful. That one individual who will complete you and give your life meaning.

She'll be the one who'll understand you like no other person at any point has or will. She will look into your eyes and see your soul. She can read your mind and think about what you need without you saying a word.

She's the one you can never find, even if you use whatever might remain of your days looking — on the grounds that she's not real. You expect romance to be like in the movies. You expect dating and having a relationship to be as easy as breathing — and whatever issues you have along the way to be resolved in the cutest conceivable manner, like in the movies. You anticipate that she should purchase a boarding pass and pursue you down the air terminal just to let you know the amount she cherishes you.

On the off chance that you're holding on until you feel an otherworldly connection with somebody before you begin putting resources into a committed relationship with them, you will be single for eternity.

13. You're overcomplicating things — inexplicably.

Most girls simply believe you should message them. Simply say "Hi."

Simply ask them out. Assuming that it works out in a good way, ask them out once more.

Stay in contact. Get some information about her day, her life, her ventures. Be keen on what her identity is.

Try not to vanish, and don't mess around. Be direct. Tell her, "I like you, and I might want to see where this goes." That's all there is to it. Adhere to the essentials and things will undoubtedly run a great deal smoother for you from here on out.

CHAPTER THREE

WHEN IS IT GOOD TO GET A GIRLFRIEND?

You googled a phrase "I want a girlfriend" and you come from a pretty dark place right now at this moment. You are feeling down, imagining that the issues you have will be fixed by a girlfriend.

Furthermore, I know how you feel. I've been there numerous times. However, before you bounce into it, listen to me for several minutes. Sadly, buddy, I'm here to let you know that your concerns presumably will not be fixed by getting another girlfriend. As a matter of fact, here are reasons you really want to think about first prior to going into any relationship and getting a girlfriend.

Despite the fact that you may be nodding your head in disagreement at the moment, you will be thankful for this counsel later. Since it will keep you from getting a girlfriend for some unacceptable reasons. Furthermore, a relationship on insecure establishments is ill-fated to end quickly. Truth be told, we as a whole know how much breakup hurt so we should simply keep that all along.

So read these reasons you need to consider prior to getting a girlfriend first, and afterward choose if you truly need a girlfriend at this moment.

1. Are you making a decision from a high point, not a low point

This doesn't have to be significant just to the "getting a girlfriend" circumstance. This is the kind of thing you ought to rehearse for each significant part of your life. What's more, getting a girlfriend is certainly one of them.

So, what's the significance here? It implies that you don't make a choice when you are at a depressed spot in life. Since that normally implies that your judgment is blurred by your ongoing profound state.

Also, at low point in your life, you are feeling sort of crappy. In getting what is going on, this would be the point at which you are on a dance floor at some party and everybody has a young lady to move to with the exception of you. At that point, you feel alone or you feel rage, shame, outrage, dissatisfaction and essentially not generally excellent.

Any choice you make at that point is a result of your ongoing bad profound state-and by that, you make sure that the choice isn't something you truly care about. It is basically a response. You ought to settle on a conclusion about getting a girlfriend in an encouraging climate, where you are completely relaxed and when you can really see plainly why you really want or needn't bother with a girlfriend. It perhaps sounds ludicrous to you at this moment; however, these simple methods are strong past creative mind. You should simply follow up on them.

2. Do you have any idea what you look for?

Getting a girlfriend is a quiet inquiry to respond to. You basically say yes or no. Yet, the response to the inquiry "What sort of girlfriend you look for" is a truly difficult one.

Since here you really want to depict your ideal girlfriend, let yourself know what she resembles, how she smells, what she cherishes and doesn't adore, her little peculiarities and ticks which you will adore and despise simultaneously.

Alright, I'm getting a smidgen more into the subtleties than I ought to however you get the point.

She wants to have a similar worth framework as you do which doesn't imply that you want to do exactly the same thing. Be that as it may, she should have the option to grasp you.

Be that as it may, here is the trick.

For you to understand what she will be, you want to understand what you need. Furthermore, for you to understand what you need, you want to investigate yourself. To investigate yourself, you really want to become mindful of what your identity is, what you need to become, what are your fantasies and dreams for the future, how you envision your ideal world and in that, where does a girlfriend fit in.

These are intense inquiries that you really want to reply, however they are fulfilling. Furthermore, after you know what your identity is and what you believe should do throughout everyday life, you can without much of a stretch understand why you need a girlfriend in your life and on the off chance that you do, what sort of a girlfriend.

3. Are you taking in social pressure from friends and family?

Despite the fact that the vast majority of the enlightened world lives uninhibitedly, we are as yet impacted by our way of life, guardians, grandparents and the climate we are a piece of. There is no doubt. In any case, on the off chance that you are getting a girlfriend just to satisfy somebody who might be listening or fulfill a social standard, then if it's not too much trouble, stop. You are giving yourself and your girlfriend a raw deal and it will simply prompt a bad relationship which will either wind up as a separation or more terrible - end up as a bad marriage.

So, on the off chance that you are constrained to get a girlfriend, tell everybody quietly to f*** off and do whatever you might want to do.

4. Are you suffering from loneliness or aloneness?

There is a major distinction in these two. Loneliness is the inaccessibility of individuals to speak with on any level. Aloneness, be that as it may, is the inaccessibility of somebody to speak with at your degree of mindfulness.

Most guys are attempting to tackle aloneness by applying answers for loneliness. You know those guys who just starting with one girlfriend then onto the next, continuously having somebody close but never having them stick.

Indeed, that is the situation of somebody attempting to tackle aloneness or their inability to find somebody who can understand them by utilizing arrangements that address forlornness or basically having another person there. What's more, for this situation, nobody is now and again better compared to somebody.

At the point when you simply need a girlfriend since you would rather not feel alone, then, at that point, by definition you mustn't get a girlfriend. That is the time you want to use to investigate yourself and sort out why you feel like that.

At the point when you tackle the issue of depression, then, at that point, you will be allowed to find a genuine connection, somebody who can figure you out. And afterward, and really at that time, will be the ideal opportunity to track down a girlfriend.

5. Do you know your life's needs?

Getting a girlfriend to simply get a girlfriend is an issue itself. At the point when you have your life's needs fixed, then, at that point, you can find a girlfriend which squeezes into that image. The need number 1 in your life ought to never be your girlfriend. It ought to be your vision, mission and life's motivation.

Allow me just to separate this a smidgen.

You don't need a girlfriend, you need what you figure a girlfriend will give you. Furthermore, that is bliss and satisfaction. Yet, truth be told the main spot you will find genuine bliss and satisfaction in your life is in you.

At the point when you sort out what you need to do, that will be your directing star throughout everyday life and you will seek after it. Also, that will be your need throughout everyday life. At the point when you simply need a girlfriend for having a girlfriend, you will get lost on your way. That generally prompts separations and hopelessness overall. Since you no longer know who you really are.

Yet, by having your motivation in line and seeking after it as vital throughout everyday life, you will find an extraordinary girlfriend which squeezes into that sort of way of life.

6. Did you attempt some fish in the ocean?

By the examination of numerous positive psychologists like Martin Seligman and Daniel Gilbert, we are absolutely silly with regards to figuring what will fulfill us.

We assume we need something and that it will make us cheerful and just when we to get it, we sort out that it didn't satisfy us. Much more terrible, it caused us to feel way unhappier on the grounds that now there is nothing to take a stab at and we want to reexamine ourselves. At the point when you assume you need a girlfriend and a girlfriend with precisely these sorts of advantages and qualities, you may be so off-base and you didn't have any acquaintance with it.

So, the best thing is to really go out there and see what you like. Try not to go into a profound, serious relationship when you are 17 and think that "this is all there is to it!" You haven't even seen what is out there nor what you genuinely like. You don't have anything to compare it with.

It took me years to sort out what I truly need in a girlfriend and that was generally sorting out what is it that I truly care about. You want to investigate yourself with others to sort out what you truly need so perhaps getting a girlfriend right currently isn't the most ideal move. You ought to evaluate casual relationships with young ladies to see what you like and abhorrence so you really understand what you are keen on.

7. Do you adore yourself?

This is a major one since you will be like "what sort of inquiry is this? Obviously that I love myself." However truly a great many people really don't. The vast majority are looking for another person, their "soul mates" to satisfy them, to provide them meaning and a motivation. The vast majority don't adore themselves so they are frantically attempting to find somebody who might be listening will give them the adoration they can't give to themselves.

Furthermore, when they really do find a girlfriend out there, somebody who is in an equivalent quest for somebody who they would cherish in light of the fact that they can't do it for themselves, then, at that point, those individuals make a reliant relationship.

One individual is generally a casualty and the other one is a hero. One individual needs to put all the fault on themselves to feel deserving of affection while the other continually needs to save somebody to feel deserving of adoration.

These sorts of relationship are ill-fated to fizzle.

So, pose yourself the inquiry "Am I getting a girlfriend since I maintain that somebody should cherish me?" On the off chance that the response to this question is yes, you shouldn't get a girlfriend.

8. Do you really want a girlfriend or a rebound?

In the event that you just got out from a long-term relationship, then you totally needn't bother with another girlfriend. You, friend, need to flirt with a rebound.

You have recently invested such a lot of energy with an individual and didn't wind up well. Regardless of who split it up, there are still such countless annoying issues and lingering feelings lying around.

So most importantly, it would be out of line to some other young lady on the off chance that you just hopped with her in another relationship. Any girlfriend would rather not share their person with another person, particularly while the sting of the past relationship is still so strong. Thinking about that, you simply need some alone and amazing time! Furthermore, there is nothing out of sorts in having casual hookups, simply regularly practice something different. So, inquire as to whether you really want and need a girlfriend at this moment, or could a rebound and a casual hookup get the job done?

9. Is it true that you are prepared to focus on one?

This is for you compulsive workers out there. A girlfriend isn't a masturbation gadget. It's an individual with its wants and needs and you really want to ready to satisfy them.

Focusing on a girlfriend means carving out the opportunity to be seeing someone. Assuming you are accustomed to contemplating your arrangements for summer and excursions, having spare energy to do various things, haphazardly investigating things - well that should be viewed as now.

If you have any desire to focus on a girlfriend, you should really try to understand that your time presently should be imparted to your girlfriend. What's more, this is the sort of thing a considerable lot of us sort of don't need. Since a relationship isn't consistently rainbows and butterflies, it's persistent effort! Despite the fact that it's worth the effort, you really want to assign time to it.

What's more, on the off chance that you are the person who is master time manager or simply partake in your freedom an excessive lot, you want to re-read the rundown above. Since, supposing that you are forfeiting your time and opportunity, then, at that point, you should be certain that this young lady is the right sort of girlfriend.

10. Do you really need to impart your life to somebody?

This is the last thing on our list since the above reasons are all essentials for this one. At the end of the day, having a girlfriend means imparting your life to another person. In addition to the beneficial things, yet the bad things also. Being there when it's the hardest for you, however for her too implies a great deal.

You are sharing all that you are with another person and it feels freeing and unnerving simultaneously. Certain individuals are never prepared for this, feeling that the other individual won't adore them for who they genuinely are. So, they conceal so, futile connections and keep away from any sort of profound relationship.

Furthermore, frankly with you, you won't presumably ever be prepared for something like this. There will continuously be a touch of doubt regardless of how extraordinary your girlfriend is. Yet, the stunt here is to think and go through the trepidation.

In the event that you will share all that you are with another person and stick around, then, at that point, you ought to get a girlfriend. Yet, to come here takes such a lot of work and tragically, that work should be done alone.

Jim Rohn said it the best " The best gift you can give someone is your very own personal development. I used to say, "If you will take care of me, I will take care of you. "Now I say, I will take care of me for you, if you will take care of you for me." I accept you figured out how to find your solution in these reasons and that it will assist you with pursuing the most ideal choice.

CHAPTER FOUR

KEY THINGS TO CONSIDER BEFORE STARTING THE PROCESS OF GETTING A GIRLFRIEND

Getting a girlfriend is definitely not a hugely troublesome accomplishment to accomplish. I figured out how to succeed, and I was only an ordinary person. Be that as it may, it'll challenge you. Also, the more you know, the good you'll be.

On the off chance that you're prepared for a girlfriend in your life, this is the final aide you'll ever require ever again.

Step #1: Get Your Attitude Right

The absolute first thing you want to do is get your headspace right as a man. You want to take on areas of strength for a, manly casing, and begin living like a genuine extremely confident man. Presently, few out of every odd man will be alpha, and that checks out. You might be an independent person, similar to a sigma male. Or on the other hand, you might be a moderately 'typical' fellow, similar to the delta male. One way or the other, understanding one thing is inconceivably significant. You really want to even out up to improve as a man. This is the first and most significant stage on the way to prevailing at getting a girlfriend who'll show valid, genuine, consuming sexual craving for you.

Step #2: Don't Be Frantic for Ladies to like You

The excitement of being seen, recognized, perhaps getting a beautiful grin from an exquisite Lady!

To lay it out plainly, you need to get away from the world view limited by fear, and take on a mentality of genuine sexual overflow. Men who are 'frantic' for ladies to like them radiate strong low worth markers — while high worth men who are chasing after their motivation throughout everyday life and endeavoring to have an enduring effect in the universe emit strong high worth markers. This is unquestionably significant, on the grounds that lovely ladies are just really inspired by high worth men.

Step #3: Work on Turning into a High Worth Man

Turning into a high worth man is a deep-rooted pursuit. In any case, you can begin today by adjusting your mentality, stepping up your body, expanding your procuring potential, and teaching yourself.

Begin heading out to the gym. Begin perusing a few quality books. Begin paying attention to some extraordinary digital broadcasts.

As such, begin genuinely evening out up to turn into the best man you might potentially be. However, you don't need to totally prevail by any means of this to begin dating. However long you're beginning, investing the energy, and have an arrangement for your future, you're doing great. In any case, a fair warning — you ought to never allow ladies to disrupt your own excursion as a man. As a man, you should push forward and turn into your best self that you might potentially be. That should be your primary goal, consistently. However, as your dating marketplace value increases, you'll find that all of this personal development will give you a gigantic major advantage over the dating scene.

Step #4: Put on Your High-Worth Uniform

Prior to going out to meet individuals, make friends, build relationships, and meet wonderful ladies, it's critical to get your look made certain about. Furthermore, that implies putting various outfits together that guarantee that regardless of what day of the week it is, assuming you go out, you'll be looking fine as hell. The last thing you need is to meet somebody significant (or a super-hot lady) looking like a good-for-nothing who just carried up. So put some thought into what kinds of garments look best on you, and begin assembling a few outfits so that you'll continuously have one prepared.

Figure out how to dress for your body type, so you can look great paying little mind to what shape you're presently in.

Step #5: Extend Your Groups of friends

In any case, the most compelling thing to recollect is this:

You should proactively, naturally extend your groups of friends to meet ladies. That implies accepting things that individuals welcome you to, and assuming a sense of ownership with tracking down fun, social activities (either with your young men, or without anyone else) two or three days of the week.

Step #6: Develop Alpha Male Confidence

Okay. You're dealing with your outlook, you're dressing like a genuine modern courteous fellow, and you're extending your groups of friends. Assuming you're getting things done as needs be, in the end you will run into some cuties. Presently, now is the right time to begin nailing the 5 fundamental dating abilities. In any case, everything begins with a sound portion of extremely alpha man confidence.

Ladies are keen on mysterious, influential men who trust in themselves. They're not intrigued by men who have no confidence, charisma, or self-esteem.

Step #7: Utilize the 5 Overall Dating Abilities to Ask Ladies on Dates

These abilities will take you from zero to legend assuming you figure out how to accurately utilize them. Without a doubt, this will be a very essential outline. However, the thoughts are basic. Monitoring how the progression of the commitment is going is the way to remaining on the money and keeping away from a slowdown. Most men who battle to get dates get balanced up on at least one of these abilities — so the more you practice them, and the more you get at flawlessly progressing through them, the more you'll get at consistently moving toward ladies, connecting with them, and effectively asking them out. Everything begins with the approach.

- *Approach*

The approach step is the beginning of the cycle, and happens before you say anything. It conceals strolling to her, looking certain, looking comparable to conceivable, and establishing a strong first connection. The main thing about moving toward a lady is to ensure that your non-verbal communication is spot on.

In any case, the fundamentals are as the following:

Be very much prepared and sharp looking

Approach with confidence

Visually engage

Make certain of yourself

Don't hold back, act intimidated, or act 'scared' of her

Stay cheerful, your shoulders back, and your spine straight

Furthermore, in particular — don't worship her or deal with her like she's superior to you. That is a one-way-pass to 'unsexy' town.

- *Engage*

This is one of the most over-examined pieces of the whole dating process. A few men will attempt to retain and go through pickup lines or schedules. In any case, truth be told, the most ideal way to attract a lady is simply to be your incredible self. I normally get going with a fast introduction, understood quickly by the justification for why I'm drawing in with her in the first place.

The following are a couple of instances of 'openers' I've utilized with ladies previously, and they generally ended up successfully:

"Hi. I am Josh. What's your name?"

"Hello, I go by Josh. You most likely get this constantly; however, I need to inquire. Could I at any point get your number?"

I certainly don't overthink it when I present myself and draw in with ladies. What's more, frankly, that appears to work the best. Offering a decent, confident handshake can likewise be an incredible commendation to the hello.

Generally, you maintain that the commitment should be proficient — however you would like to try to visually connect, and to make an honest effort to ooze manly sexual energy.

Obviously, you believe she should feel that you're into her without coming right out and say it.

- *Build Connection*

After you've acquainted yourself with her, it'll be an ideal opportunity to begin a discussion of some sort or another. Clearly, the subject, profundity, and state of mind of this discussion will be directed by the unique circumstance. However, the significant thing to recollect is that you would rather not get slowed down on casual conversation. It couldn't be any more obvious, connection is a strong antecedent to sexual attraction for ladies. Furthermore, the most effective way to build connection with a lady is to take the discussion from 'non-personal' to 'personal' as fast as could be expected. This is generally achieved by posing her real inquiries about her life, thoughts, side interests, convictions, and so forth. At the end of the day — simply attempt to get to know her a tad. Assuming that she asks you inquiries consequently, open up and share a few responses about yourself. Being weak closes what I call the 'connection loop,' and produces a more profound degree of trust and closeness.

- *Sexually Escalate*

While asking a lady out in, you're presumably not going to sexually escalate excessively. A tiny amount makes a huge difference at this beginning phase of the game. However, you really do have to physically heighten, on the grounds that this lets her in exceptionally clear language know that you're physically keen on her.

Furthermore, that is a truly significant piece of the cycle that a ton of men battle with. On the off chance that you don't do this effectively, she might regard the communication as an endeavor at friendship, and continue to friendzone you.

For instance:

In the event that I saw a lady at the shopping mall and concluded that I needed to ask her out, I'd:

Move toward her with confidence (approach)

Present myself (engage)

Begin some casual conversation (engage)

Pose her two or three inquiries to get to know her (build connection)

Physically heighten gently by being a flirt a tiny bit, and afterward touching her arm somewhat (sexually escalate)

Then, go in for the close — which for this situation, would be me getting her number or potentially requesting that she get a coffee with me later (close)

Furthermore, I'd hurry up. No doubt, all of this would occur in the range of under 5 minutes.

As such, sexually escalating while asking ladies out or getting their number is an inconspicuous workmanship. Oozing manly sexual confidence, participating in a touch of being a flirt, and using a tiny measure of actual contact is normally sufficient to get the job done.

Closing is the piece of the cycle where you request the number, or ask her out on the date.

During this part, you should stay certain. You really want to accept that she will say yes, and act appropriately.

Why? Because you want her to feel at ease.

My number one method for exploring this is to simply be normal about it.

I'll typically express something like this:

"Hello, it was incredible meeting you. I need to go, yet I'd very much want to hang out at some point. Allow me to get your number."

Right now, I'd take out my telephone, totally anticipating that she should be calm with giving me her number, and continue to type it in as she gives it to me.

You generally need to accept she will say yes.

Pro tip: You'll get a 'yes' on a more regular basis in the event that you make her to respond to 'yes' to one more inquiry prior to asking for the number

Step #8: Defeat Your Approach Anxiety

A ton of men battle with approach tension. They're hesitant to approach ladies and begin a discussion.

Yet, here's reality. The least complex method for beating it is to make it happen. At the point when I initially began figuring out how to move toward ladies, I gave myself a standard.

I needed to move toward a specific number of ladies consistently, and ask them for their number.

This got me out of the propensity for fearing dismissal, and got me into the propensity for enjoying connecting with beautiful ladies, paying little heed to what the result would have been. I conversed with fast-food workers, waitresses, women at coffee shops, women at the bookstore, women at the club, women at the grocery store — any place ladies were to be found, I'd be drawing nearer and beginning discussions.

Also, prepare to have your mind blown. It worked.

Of course, I got a ton of 'no' replies. However, the more practice I got, the more I began to get more 'yes' reactions consistently.

It couldn't be any more obvious, assuming you never ask, you won't ever succeed. I'll be straightforward with you.

Few out of every odd endeavor to ask a lady out will end with a 'yes.' You will confront some dismissal.

However, that is Fine.

As a man, your mindset about dismissal ought to be a positive one. It's smarter to be dismissed multiple times than to never take care of business and inquire. So, assuming you get a 'no,' that is completely fine. Hold your head high, grin, say thanks to her for her time, and go about your business. You just got some free practice, which'll make you substantially more liable to get a 'yes' the following time you attempt.

Step #9: Narrow Down Your Choices

You're likely beginning to notice that one of them is beginning to stand apart as a true complement to your life. She'll stand apart as your number one. She simply gets you better than the others. The sex is better, she's hotter, she's not showing any warnings, she's more amusing to spend time with, you coexist with her loved ones — and you're beginning to think that dating 'different ladies' is simply time squandered, on the grounds that you'd prefer to be investing that energy with her than with any other person. Gentleman, this is the manner by which you'll realize that you've probably tracked down the 'girlfriend' young lady.

This is the way to continue.

- *Escalate to a Relationship*

The absolute most significant thing to comprehend about this indispensable step is that, with you being a high worth man, the lady ought to continuously enter your frame. Furthermore, the absolute first illustration of this is that the lady ought to constantly be the one to start the 'where do we stand' talk. Assuming you start this discussion rather than her, it'll get the whole relationship going with you attempting to enter her edge. That might satisfy her for the time being. Yet, in the long haul, it'll compromise her regard for you as a high worth man. Conceivably, you'll radiate low-esteem markers assuming you're the person who brings it up. So, this is the way, as a man, you ought to heighten the relationship.

Step #10: Keep on focusing on Your Development as a Man

Indeed, even at this phase of the game, you should never focus on this lady over things like:

Developing your business

Heading out to the gym

Investing energy with your friends

Doing things you appreciate and think often about

This will assist with setting the fact that, despite the fact that you two are developing close relationship with the eventual result of settling on arrangements, you're as yet your own man — you actually anticipate that she should enter your frame, not the opposite way around. Try not to fall into the snare of making her the mission. Your main goal is dependably your motivation and your development as a man.

Step #11: Show Your Expanded Interest in Her by Focusing on Her over Different Ladies

As you begin to ask her on additional dates, have more sleepovers, do more activities with her, and give her more admittance to 'inside' your life, you'll likewise be removing different ladies out of the image. These different ladies won't fill your need any longer, and they'll ultimately be supplanted by this high-esteem lady with whom you can see a genuine relationship shaping.

Depend on it, she'll see this. You won't need to express anything about it. She'll become mindful of it. Also, assuming she's keen on exactly the same thing, this will make her need to develop nearer to you, and she'll be exceptionally grateful that she's getting such a large amount your attention.

Step #12: Keep on living Like a single Man until She Raises 'The Discussion'

Presently, here a ton of men truly wallow and fizzle.

Here is reality, men. Indeed, you might like her, and she might be your number one.

However, until she starts a serious 'where do we stand talk' with you, she's NOT your better half, and doesn't get girlfriend 'freedoms' as far as you might be concerned, your time, your space, or your needs. You should keep on carrying on with your life as a single man. You should keep on pursuing your motivation. You should proceed to just give her the space of 'the young lady you're casually dating' in your life, not the full 'girlfriend space.' In the long run, assuming she truly needs you, this will force her to need to secure you, so she doesn't lose you. Furthermore, that is the point at which she'll have the discussion with you. On the off chance that she isn't headed to have 'the discussion' with you, something's off-base — and you'd be better off to keep her in the 'casual dating' space.

Step #13: Settle on Arrangements

Congrats. You've made some amazing progress. You began with bettering yourself and turning into a higher worth man. You've extended your groups of friends, conquer approach nervousness, and began dating a few wonderful ladies. Furthermore, presently, your number one young lady has put you down and posed a vital inquiry.

"All in all, what are we?"

"Are we officially boyfriend and girlfriend?"

"I want to make this official. Can we have 'the talk'?"

Congrats. This high worth, wonderful lady really maintains wants you and wants should be your girlfriend. Yet, there's another significant stage. Each serious relationship comprises of arrangements you make with each other. What's more, right now, you might have to talk about some guidelines. You might need to converse with her about things like:

Will you be monogamous?

What kinds of things will you really want from one another to be in a serious relationship?

Can you both give each other the balance of freedom and domestic overlap required to make a relationship possible?

Furthermore, maybe above all: would she say she will enter your frame and become a more private piece of your life?

This doesn't need to be a very difficult or in-depth talk, and you may both simply need to voice your most pressing prerequisites for the present. You'll most likely arrange and go with arrangements constantly all through the relationship as it advances, and that is something worth being thankful for. Yet, all in the interim, there's another thing that you really want to do, as a man.

Step #16: Take care of business of Trustworthiness

It's easy to be a guy, but it takes courage, integrity, character, honor, strength, discipline, and humility to be a man. – Burk Parsons

All in all, don't be the sort of man who says a certain something, and does another. Try not to be the sort of man who can't be relied on to satisfy the arrangements he's made with his girlfriend. If you don't want to consent to something, don't. Furthermore, all the same, likewise be firm in holding her to the arrangements that she's made. Furthermore, recollect this. You ought to never persevere with a lady who doesn't satisfy her end of the arrangements.

One last suggestion:

Make sure to keep on pursuing greatness, step up, and seek after your motivation as a man.

Getting a girlfriend is a major move in life, and it tends to be loads of fun. In any case, it ought to never be the all-out focal point of your life and energy. Go with effortlessness, my friends, and never surrender your power.

FAQs

How can I make a girl fall in love with me?

You can't in fact ' make a woman fall in love with you '. Yet you can build its chances happening naturally. How? By stepping up and turning into a genuine high-esteem man. Ladies are searching for that. What's more, the nearer you get to that imprint, the simpler it'll be to stand out enough to be noticed by high-esteem, beautiful ladies.

How do you ask a girl to be your girlfriend?

As a high worth man, it isn't to your greatest advantage to start the 'girlfriend/boyfriend' conversation. Keep carrying on with life as a single man, and embrace single sexual overflow until your #1 young lady sits you down and attempts to 'secure you' with a 'where do we stand' talk. Then, at that point, you choose if you're prepared to focus on this lady or not. It's just straightforward.

How would you get a girlfriend over text?

In addition to the fact that men never start should the 'girlfriend/boyfriend' discussion, yet they should Never under any circumstance start it through text. This sort of thing ought to constantly happen eye to eye. Text informing ought to fill just three needs during the dating system:

1. Text momentarily to orchestrate physical dates

2. Text to check-in, flirt, and make casual conversation over the course of the day (when you begin seeing each other on a more ordinary premise)

3. Text to pose check-in, flirt, and make small talk (like what time you're getting together, or to tell her that you're behind schedule)

Important discussions ought to never happen through text.

CHAPTER FIVE

WAYS TO GET A GIRLFRIEND

1. Putting Your Best self forward

Wear garments that help you have a positive outlook on yourself. Go through your storeroom and select garments that fit you well. Flaunt what your identity is, like your inclinations or character. This will assist you with having high expectations about yourself so you can do your absolute best. Try not to stress over your body type since everybody is alluring in their own particular manner. For example, pick something like a concert and pants, a button-up shirt and khakis, or cowhide and denim. In the event that you're womanlier, you could pick pastels or botanical prints. You could flaunt your inclinations by wearing shirts including your #1 groups or sports pullovers from your #1 group.

Practice great individual cleanliness to make yourself really engaging. Wash no less than one time each day, clean your teeth two times per day, and utilize individual consideration items like antiperspirant. Moreover, ensure your garments are washed. This will assist you with seeming your best and will show young ladies that you take great consideration of yourself. You don't have to drench yourself in cologne or do any manscaping, except if that is the very thing that you need.

Do fun exercises or a side interest so you appear to be fascinating. Make a rundown of things you like to do and themes that interest you. Then, do something like something fun consistently. This will assist you with partaking in your life more and will show young ladies that you're a fascinating individual. For example, figure out how to play an instrument, join a games group, take up painting, or join a bar test group. Tip: After you're in a relationship, critical that you proceed with these side interests. A healthy relationship permits the two individuals to invest energy dealing with themself.

Be alright with being distant from everyone else so you seem certain. On the off chance that you appear to be desperate and needy, you might struggle with making an association with individuals. Search for ways of being cheerful while you're single. Invest energy doing things that premium you, and partake in your experience with friends. Try not to make tracking down a relationship the main thing in your life. List justifications for why it's great to be single so you don't feel terrible. For example, you get to invest more energy with your friends, you possess more energy for your leisure activities, and you can converse with various young ladies to see what you like. Individuals are more drawn to you when you appear to be content with your life, so this can assist you with getting a girlfriend.

2. Meeting Young ladies

Request that your friends acquaint you with young ladies they know. Your companions probably know young ladies they could acquaint you with, and this is a typical way for individuals to meet. Get your friends to orchestrate bunch excursions so you can meet their female friends. Variation: On social media, interact with girls who comment on your friends' posts. Answer the remarks to check whether the young lady will converse with you. Assuming she does, friend or follow her.

Join clubs or groups to meet young ladies at school. Search for an after-school club that seems fun or go for a games group. Go to club gatherings, occasions, or games to meet more individuals. Attempt to befriend young ladies you meet with the goal that you can track down an expected girlfriend. On the off chance that you find a young lady you like, welcome her to accomplish something club-or group related so you can get to know each other. For example, suppose you're in debate club together. You could say, "Would you like to meet at the bistro tomorrow to analyze cases?"

Go to occasions to meet more young ladies. On the off chance that you're in school, go to occasions like school moves, football match-ups, and plays. As another choice, hit up nearby occasions like shows, celebrations, or meetups to meet young ladies. Attempt to befriend the young ladies you meet by beginning a discussion about the occasion. If a young lady would appear to not like to talk, continue on toward another young lady. At last, you'll make another friend. You can track down open occasions on Facebook, Meetup.com, or local news sites

Propose to assist a young lady with something. Helping out can be a decent icebreaker to present yourself. Notice in the event that a young lady is by all accounts battling with something, offer your help. Assuming she acknowledges your assistance, present yourself and check whether she'll converse with you. Say, "I'm Alex. How's your day going?"

They probably shouldn't talk, and that is fine. To leave, simply say, "The pleasure is all mine" and leave.

Attempt internet dating assuming you're 18 or older. The incredible part about online dating is that everybody is there for a similar explanation. Message young ladies who have comparable interests to you, and chat with them a piece prior to asking them out for coffee. Remember that it's generally expected to message a ton of young ladies before somebody answers. Make an effort not to think about it literally in light of the fact that everybody encounters exactly the same thing.

3. Intriguing a Young lady

Pose inquiries to become familiar with a young lady who intrigues you. Converse with her about herself, and show real interest in her response. Gesture along as she talks, and ask follow up inquiries to find out more. This will show her that you're keen on her identity personally. Pose inquiries like, "What do you like to do for fun?" "What are your objectives for the following 5 years?" or "What's the most interesting thing that has at any point happened to you?"

Center around young ladies who share things for all intents and purpose with you. A young lady will be keener on being your girlfriend in the event that you share things practically speaking. Pick young ladies who have comparative interests, leisure activities, or character attributes as you do. They needn't bother with to be precisely similar to you, yet having shared conviction is significant. For example, you could both play a similar instrument or both appreciate games. Everybody needs to be seen, heard, and acknowledged for what their identity is.

At the point when you show a young lady that you are truly intrigued by what she cherishes, it causes her to feel that you care about her. Try not to claim to share something practically speaking with a young lady to definitely stand out. This generally misfires since she'll ultimately acknowledge you were not frank.

Offer veritable commendations to young ladies who interest you. This will help her have a positive outlook on herself and it shows her you might keen on be more than friends. Educate her something decent regarding herself and make an effort not to zero in on her body. Just offer 1 commendation at a time so she doesn't get awkward. You could say, "Extraordinary response in class today," "Your exhibition was astounding!" or "This shirt is great."

Flaunt your awareness of what's actually funny by making wisecracks and stories. Everybody likes to laugh, so utilizing humor can make a young lady like you more. Gain a couple of jokes from the Web and contemplate the most interesting things that have happened to you. At the point when you're around the young lady you like, share these entertaining funny tidbits with her or your group of friends. Indeed, even terrible jokes can be interesting assuming you focus on the zinger. Make it a point to giggle at your own jokes and simply be senseless.

4. Asking a Young lady Out

Hint that you want a date by asking her to do a fun activity. This will show her you're intrigued without you having to state it straightforwardly. Notice the movement and inquire as to whether she's keen on it. On the off chance that she says OK, recommend you hang out. On the off chance that she's not intrigued, propose something you realize she prefers. In the event that she actually says she's not intrigued, it's ideal to continue on. For example, say, "The championship game is coming up and I'm pondering going. Are you interested?" As another example, say, "It's been forever since I went bowling. What about you?"

Be direct and request a date in the event that you feel courageous. Being direct is the most ideal way to get a date, however you might be dismissed. Let the young lady know that you're keen on going out with her, then recommend a date.

Make her feel special on the date by showing her attention. Your date is your opportunity to establish a decent connection with her. Be good to her, and really focus the whole time. Here are some ways to show her you give it a second thought: Keep your phone set aside, pose her a ton of inquiries, look at her without flinching while she's talking, ask her how she's doing, Offer her compliments.

Request a second date toward the end from the evening. Tell her you had a good time and need to see her once more. Then, follow up with your date with a text or call to tell her you had a good time. Say, "I'd very much want to take you out once more." You can likewise request the second date later, in the event that you like. For example, you could message her subsequently to say you had a good time and request the subsequent date. On the off chance that you're a grown-up, holding up a couple of days might be ideal.

Invest energy with her to assist your relationship with developing. How long you spend together face to face will rely on how old you are and your own timetable. Text her every day to stay in contact, and communicate via social media, in the event that you both use it. Give a valiant effort to plan customary dates or home bases, regardless of whether you're simply seeing each other at school. Furthermore, really try to sit by her when you're in a class or occasion together. You'll probably go on a couple of dates or message each other for a little while before you request that she be your girlfriend. Attempt to show restraint since surging things can drive her away. Talking, messaging, and hanging out together will assist you develop your association with her, which can assist you with persuading her to be your girlfriend.

Try not to do a lot for a young lady you're attempting to date in the event that she's not investing a similar measure of energy. She may not be keen on you, so it's ideal to move on. Try not to attempt to race into a relationship. A sound relationship finds opportunity to develop and form into something genuine.

Center around carrying on with a day to day existence that you appreciate as opposed to on getting a girlfriend. This will assist you with finding love better compared to attempting to compel a relationship with somebody. Try not to discuss past connections. This is a no and a definite mood killer. You will just project the feeling that you can't give up. Try not to fly off the handle at her assuming she dismisses you. Everybody has a privilege to their own sentiments.

CHAPTER SIX

PLACES TO FIND YOUR FUTURE GIRLFRIEND AND HOW TO APPROACH HER

It's like when you leave school, there's no simple method for tracking down a girlfriend! Meeting ladies can be a test and making a connection that prompts a relationship can feel almost unthinkable.

In any case, there is a way! There is a method for meeting ladies, approach them, and follow through so that she's keen on making the following stride with you.

In this chapter, I'll show you places to find your future girlfriend and what you'll need to keep away from, basic contents for how to move toward her, and why "the conversation starter" is old and what you ought to use rather to make way for association genuinely.

I want to offer you a fool-proof pick-up line since it sounds so straightforward, so natural, so proficient — one line and she's yours...

Be that as it may, it doesn't exist. A more real methodology is the best approach.

My father, John Dark, says that the most ideal way to start a discussion is to present yourself. Alright. That is sufficiently credible however where do you go from that point?

All things being equal, focus on your common environmental factors and ask her perspective on something. She doesn't have any acquaintance with you, yet everybody has an assessment and assuming that you allow her an opportunity to communicate hers and you approach it with deference, indeed, that is an incredible initial feeling.

When you approach and settle on something worth agreeing on and make her discussion, it's the ideal opportunity for you to go through the pick-up line's replacement and it's called:

Follow Through- An incredible discussion isn't sufficient to get you a girlfriend; you need to make a reason for future association and that is the very thing that the Follow Through does. So, for every area and move toward strategy, I'm likewise going to give you a content for how to See everything through to completion.

Places to Avoid meeting Women and Why

You might associate with ladies in these spots yet I don't prescribe moving toward them with the aim to make them your girlfriend. Here's the reason:

A Club or Bar: A lady's guards are up at a bar scene or party. It very well may be more straightforward for you to get up the boldness to converse with her when it's made from fluid yet it's not helpful for a true connection. Loud music, attractive garments, and liquor mean surface associations and games.

A Gym: A few ladies might feel differently however it is basically impossible that I need to be gotten when I'm sweat-soaked and focusing on working out. There is now a particularly clear association with sex — tight spandex, perspiring, breathing weighty, endorphins — that it simply appears skeevy when a person draws near. Ladies at the gym will quite often be careful. Rather than the club or gym, move toward her where she is looser and more open. Perhaps check one of these local people out:

Here's where to Track down a girlfriend

1. A Park

Do you have a dog? In the event that you do, there's your in.
Regardless of whether you're babysitting your friend's dog,
it's cool. Simply say, "Hello there. Gracious, wow, your
doggy is adorable. This is Milo. I'm watching for a friend."

Individuals who have dogs are promptly part of a
community, and she will feel happier with opening
dependent upon you. That is the point at which you can
circle back to, "My name is… "

In the event that you don't have a dog, feel free to approach
a lady and say hi to her pup. Assuming that dog begins to
sway its tail, you're in.

See everything through to completion: "This was enjoyable.
To rehash this or even go for some coffee, here's my

number. Text me and I'll call you. It would be perfect to see you once more."

Why the combo of "If you..." and "Text me and I'll call you" is correspondence gold:

At the point when you give an "If you," it gives her an unmistakable reason to message you and even gives her the words. The simpler you make it for her, the more probable she'll see everything through to completion. At the point when you give her your number, it sets her free from expecting to settle on you that moment. You're not asking her for anything so she's less inclined to think "No." When a man gives a lady his number, she can feel constrained to call him and be the pursuer. She could do without this by the same token. So, the enchanting center ground is to invite her to message you and let her in on that that will be your sign to call her and seek after her.

Truly… this is splendid. However, you need to completely finish and call her in fact!

Ladies experience passionate feelings between their ears, and that implies they need to hear your voice for a genuine bond to develop. To isolate yourself from the pack and stand apart as the person for her, this is the means by which you make it happen.

2. A Café

At the point when I was single, I used to deliberately bring my everyday schedule different undertakings to a bistro to resolve on to place myself there in the event that a charming person needed to converse with me.

I can't believe I'm distant from everyone else in doing this.

Move toward her and inquire, "May I share your table?"

Assuming that she says OK, plunk down and read your book or work on your PC. You can likewise ask her, "Is this a decent spot to study? This is my most memorable time here." Or "What's the best beverage on the menu here? What do you suggest?" Then present yourself.

A pleasant move is on the off chance that she completes her drink, you can inquire as to whether she'd like another and afterward request it for herself and take care of the check. Very easygoing. That will establish a connection!

See everything through to completion: "It was truly decent chatting with you. Here is my number if you at any point hope to meet for espresso intentionally at some point. Text me and I'll call you."

2. A Museum or Art Show

This is simple. Simply inquire, "What is your take of this piece?"

Trade a couple of lines (nothing too pretentious, be honest) and afterward present yourself. Perhaps proceed with the discussion to the following piece. Or on the other hand perhaps, in the event that you know a few stuff, stroll up and say, "I love this time span. They…blah blah blah (fun fact)." Simply don't blah blah blah for a really long time or you could lose her. This is about shared interests and asking her viewpoint so go ahead and allow this to motivate you for different local people.

See everything through to completion: "Well that was entertaining. I ordinarily need to drag my friends to these things so it was good to hang with somebody who really needs to be here. You realize there's another display occurring over at the _____, I'd very much want to take you assuming that you might want to go along with me. Consider it. Here is my number. Text me and I'll call you."

3. A Hardware Store

I'm not saying all ladies get overpowered the moment they stroll into Home Stop yet a great deal of us do. It's exceedingly difficult to get any assistance there, so on the off chance that you see a lady meandering around who appears as though she's needing assistance or exhortation, dip in. Try not to be deigning; be interested! Get some information about her task, what she really wants assistance on, empathize on the absence of "help," present yourself, and assuming that you truly like your collaboration, considerably try to assist her with the venture!

This is tied in with finding a way where you can add to her life and improve it so go ahead and allow this to rouse you for different local people and abilities of yours.

See everything through to completion: "Sounds like a cool undertaking. I'm eager to assist. Here is my number. You could message me at any point any time for counsel or then again on the off chance that you want a hand and I'll call you. It was pleasant meeting you. Ideally, we'll talk soon."

5. A Supermarket

You don't need to have much familiarity with cooking to pick a lady in a supermarket. Stick around the produce area and when you see somebody you like holding some produce, express something like, "Hello, I'm attempting to practice good eating habits however I'm bad with this stuff. Can I ask you what you're planning for that [eggplant, mushroom, papaya]? Like how to set it up?"

Presently you've opened her up. You're similar to a lost pup and her gatekeeper is loose. She can offer you guidance on the eggplant and, surprisingly, some advice in general feast. Sound cooking addresses your qualities and that is alluring. Whenever you make them talk, you can present yourself.

This approach is tied in with requesting help in a space where you may not feel so certain, where you express some receptive weakness and set up for her to sparkle and be the master. Go ahead and allow this to rouse you for different local people.

See everything through to completion: "Goodness. Much thanks. This was a great deal of help. I will take your recommendation and make an honest effort. Hello, here's my number. Text me assuming you recall, and I'll call you with the report on how it goes!"

5. Volunteering

This is an extraordinary climate to interface truly with ladies.

You're both working for a purpose beyond yourself. This is pleasant in light of the fact that it shows you are magnanimous and liberal, which is very alluring. Yet in addition it's ideal to stand out somewhere else in light of the fact that her guard will be looser.

Just say, "So how did you engage with this program?" After a discussion is started, you can introduce yourself.

This approach is tied in with working on a common project at a typical task or toward a shared objective that is greater than you two and can make it protected to bond, so go ahead and allow this to motivate you.

See everything through to completion: "Anyway, one week from now, same time? I love working with this association yet today, hanging with you, was my number one. Here is my number. Text me while you're anticipating working on a common project once more or regardless of whether you're simply needing craving ice cream and I'll call you."

CONCLUSION

Genuine Wins the Day

As a general rule, the key is to not come on strong, as a matter of fact, seem like you're not coming on by any means!

In the event that you're not requesting her number or requesting that she settle on you immediately, then, at that point, you're giving her space to consider it later, to let anything impression you made absorb.

She may not be drawn to you immediately in any case, later, when she's isolated sitting in front of the television or scrolling social media, she could recall your genuine interaction and think, "Perhaps."

And afterward text you because...why not?

Also, this moment it's your opportunity to call her and show

her what sort of boyfriend you could be.

12077692R00061